Awkward Grace

# Awkward Grace

Poems by

Mark Tulin

Cover design by Shay Culligan

ISBN: 978-1-950462-54-4

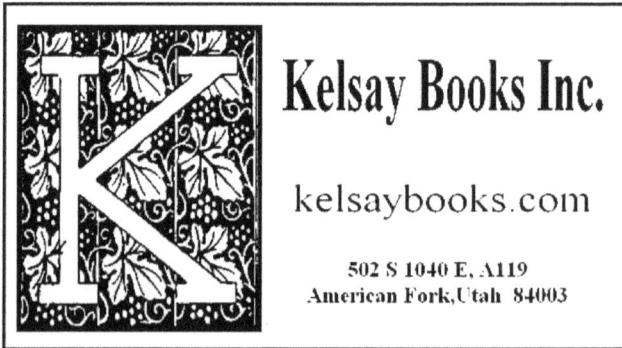

Kelsay Books Inc.

kelsaybooks.com

502 S 1040 E, A119
American Fork, Utah 84003

*To*
*Aunt Marion*

# Acknowledgments

Grateful acknowledgment is made to the editors of the following journals where these poems first appeared:

*FIVE,* Volume IV: "Broken Strings" "In and Out"
*Degenerates' Voices for Peace. Mental Health Edition* "Therapist Disease" "Pass the Cake"
*Degenerates' Voices for Peace. Homelessness Edition.* "Tattoo Man" "Christmas Day"
*elephant journal:* "The Day We Drove to Vegas"
*Vita Brevis:* "Quiet in the Park" "With Each Pose" "Awkward Grace" "Flying Kings" "Ancient Pyramid"
*Leaves of Ink:* "Caught in a Vortex" "Last Cigarette"
*Amethyst Magazine:* "Tsunami Morning"
*Literary Yard:* "Silver Throated Poet" "In the Asylum"
*Spillwords:* "Beggar's Delight" "Coffee Shop Desperado"
*The Drabble:* "The Perfect Place"
*Corvus Review,* Issue 11: "The Charmer"

Much thanks to the many friends and bloggers at Wordpress.com and Hubpages.com. Without your input, my skills would have never progressed.

I want to acknowledge all those unsheltered people that I have met on State Street, Santa Barbara who have inspired many of these poems. You amaze me with your perseverance and ingenuity.

Special thanks to my wife, Alice Tulin, for her enduring support and constructive criticism of my work. Her intuition and creativity have been a valuable resource.

And much thanks to Brian Geiger, Ivor Steven, and Tim Truzy for reading my manuscript and writing their wonderful endorsements at the back of the book.

# Contents

Last Cigarette 11

Our Familiar Spot 12

Caught in a Vortex 13

Christmas Day 15

Awkward Grace 16

Tsunami Morning 17

Behind Bookcases 19

In and Out 20

Silver Throated Poet 21

Bountiful Treasures 22

Therapist Disease 23

The Community Piano 24

Quiet of the Park 25

The Day We Drove to Vegas 26

Free Speech Table 28

Pass the Cake 29

Sandy Queen 30

The Charmer 31

Ancient Pyramid 32

Frayed Blanket 33

In the Asylum 34

The Perfect Place 36

Coffee Shop Desperado 37

Tattoo Man 38

Broken Strings 39

Waltzing Dreamers 40

Flying Kings 41

# Last Cigarette

Under the elevated train,
surrounded by steel girders
and screeching wheels,
cold water drips
down from the rafters
onto my head.

I never complain.
I never cry.
I bathe in the water,
feeling blessed
by the abandoned angels
above the dark red sky.

I watch the traffic lights
that never change.
Traffic lights
that flicker and sway
with the wind
and rain.

I hear bruised women cry,
mistreated like barking dogs.
Johns with black eyes
getting rolled by pimps
in dark alleyways.

I feel another raindrop on my dusty pate
as I hear the rumble of a passing train.
I know my life is how it's supposed to be.
I've come to accept this plight
as I take a drag from my last cigarette.

# Our Familiar Spot

We line up at church doors
accepting donations
from trusting hands
and benevolent faces.

We forage for food.
We pick through broken cans,
weed through paper bags—
bits of scraps to peck at
and eat much too fast.

We avoid men
who step on our pride,
threaten to encage us
in homeless shelters,
restrict our movement
to the fringes of the city.

But we always come back
to our familiar spot
and we never run away.
We are grateful for life's leftovers.
We hold up signs and give out flowers
to those who have sympathy.

# Caught in a Vortex

I was trapped in a brick row house,
windows with steel bars bolted shut,
caring for a woman who ate glass,
who cut my throat with her mouth,

who walked the streets naked,
asking which way to Mendocino,
barefoot and delirious,
she hitched a ride on Route 66.

But it was I who needed to escape,
run away to a place of my own,
where there were no four-point restraints
and howling wives under a full moon.

I remember the day
when I screamed at the top of my lungs,
almost impaled myself on the bedposts,
thought I had pierced the sky with my cries
and gave God a stroke.

I wished somebody could've saved me,
removed me from this house of horrors
and a wife with a toothless smile
and a hatchet in her eyes.

The story continued,
had a twisted, distorted plot.
It played out like the scratching on a chalkboard,
water torture for prisoners of war,
a crazy Edgar Allen Poe fairy tale,
lost in a spiraling vortex
unable to grab onto something.

I watched my wife get ECT.
I turned the dials, upped the ante.
She survived, though deep-fried
with her eyes bugged out
and a burnt-out glaze across the sky.

*Do you remember me?* I asked.
*No,* she said as death fell from her toasted lips
and her head broke from her neck.
Information about her past had evaporated,
only the smoky smell of brain cells
in a psychiatric hospital remained.

# Christmas Day

Whenever Christmas day rolls around,
I get nostalgic and lonely at the same time.
Joy doesn't live around here anymore.
No more one horse open sleigh or reindeer.

No Christmas carols for those laying on the dirty sidewalks.
No decorative blinking lights with angels that glow.
No smoke-blowing model trains going around the tracks.
Just a bunch of hungry souls shadowing the streets,
some stale bread, howling dogs, and bitter memories.

Where I live, there's no Santa giving gifts and bringing cheer.
No ornaments with candy canes to sweeten our lives.
No tasty Christmas meals shared with family and friends.
Just a few poor men huddled together warming their cold hands.
Just sad stories, stale cigarettes, and cheap booze in paper bags,
reeking and sleeping and coughing up our insignificant lives.

# Awkward Grace

My whole life is bound to the chair,
but I still recite my verses and rhymes.
I still share myself with the passersby
and face each day with a lyrical hope.

My life may be contained to a chair,
but I don't let the straps hold me back.
Two 12-volt batteries power my faith.
I throttle my movement with awkward grace.

My chair has become an appendage
like a protective family member.
All that I own and care about
is attached like cargo to the back of a bus.

My life may be stuck in neutral,
and my head forever cocked to the side.
My adhesive bag may be bursting full
and my muscles shaking in a Palsy spaz.

But I still have my words to read.
I still have my poetry.

# Tsunami Morning

Just like any other day,
I awoke bright and early.
I had my buttered toast,
Half & Half in my coffee.

I kissed my wife goodbye,
the dog gave a wag of his tail,
promised my twin daughters
I'd make it to their dance recital.

Opened the door and got carried away
by a big watery dinosaur.

The wave was at least a thousand feet tall,
had a wicked smile for a curl,
a destructive force of a demon crossed.

A dawn of a new era.
My old life washed away.
Good riddance to my nine-to-five job,
goodbye 401K,
I was getting tired of civilization anyway.

All my worldly possessions were gone,
my pipe dreams and gold teeth,
my daughter's roller skate key
and my silver Ford Explorer
had all floated away

Down a one-way street,
past my favorite ice-cream parlor,
past the schools I attended,
along with saturated lawyers, computer geeks,
and complete strangers I never planned to meet.

I swam submerged with the endangered species
and non-denominational types with their hipster friends.
Sadly enough, only a few people floated to the top—
a Hatha yoga instructor named Laura,
a canonized Saint from Walla Walla,
and an investment broker from Kalamazoo.

# Behind Bookcases

The tired and wounded
limp into the free library,
huddle around Fiction,
scatter among Biography,
dwell in the beauty of Poetry,
reciting Whitman and Elliot
as drool falls from their lips.

The tired and wounded
need a refuge, a shelter from the war,
to dress their gashes in prose or verse,
forgetting about their battles,
the presidents they voted for,
the God who promised
to change their lives.

They are in the corners
kneeling quietly, hardly breathing,
snot dripping from their noses;
their lives like oozing sores.

They camouflage behind bookcases,
cower in the halls and the restroom stalls.
They seek a reprieve, an honorable discharge
from the challenges they incur.

They just want to be left to roam.
To exist without contempt.
To heal their nasty wounds.
To wipe their grief on their tattered sleeves.

# In and Out

Sailor caps and frying machines,
double doubles and protein burgers—
*Can I take your order, please?*
Hand cut potatoes and onion rings,
thin beef patties with lettuce and tomato.

*Number 44, your order is ready.*
Cheese melts into the roll.
The smiling young man hands a customer the tray.

Thick milk shakes in the California sun,
hamburger heaven and crooked arrows,
palm trees with Coca-Cola eyes.
*Can I take your order please?*

# Silver Throated Poet

I once dreamed of sleeping
with a silver throated poet,
a naked siren
of verses and rhymes.

I dreamt she was the goddess of words
and kissed her with my Joyce Carrol Oats mind.
I nibbled her neck as D. H. Lawrence looked on,
encouraging her to whisper to me
in sonnets and soliloquies.

Ferlinghetti and Ginsberg gave the beats
in a cool and jazzy rhythmic flow
while I made some raunchy comments
much like the Charles Bukowski kind.

The silver throated poet moaned with pleasure
as I recalled the works of Keats,
and got kinky when it was E.E. Cummings turn
to kiss the other cheek.

Allusions and alliterations,
metaphors that left us reeling,
free verse that had no ending,
smoking cigarettes under a crescent moon,
embracing my silver throated poet;
we were never at a loss for words.

# Bountiful Treasures

He smiles when he opens the dumpster lid.
He admires all of its bountiful treasures,
rich with hidden secrets,
tokens and trinkets from childhood.

He keeps foraging
before the tenants wake up,
hoping to find something precious,
perhaps his redemption.

He pulls out a pen,
a child's toy, an old wooden flute.
He places them in his cart,
a vehicle, a conduit for hope.

All he ever wanted
was to own something
that would give him an identity.
It doesn't have to be brand new.

When the sun rises,
people pull open their blinds
along with their disapproving stares
in the cool of the early morning fog.

He knows he has to move on
to another street, a different driveway.
He gently closes the lid of the dumpster
and all the valuables left behind.

# Therapist Disease

Always seeing people's flaws too clearly,
I have the psychotherapist
disease.

I diagnose
everyone I meet:
this one has OCD,
that one with bipolar,

always losing sight
of my flaws
and my own diagnostic
categories.

# The Community Piano

Every day, I sit at the community piano
that rests in the middle of a busy sidewalk
and pretend to play like Billy Joel,
popular songs that everyone knows.

I play for the tips as the crowd shuffles by,
tapping the sticky keys for everyone but me,
blocking out the voices in my head,
and the whispers that shame and demean.

I keep playing until the black crows
stop cawing and scatter from the trees.
Until the street lights go dim and the shops close
and only a few souls are left walking alone.

I flex my cramped fingers and circle my head,
pull the wooden cover over the piano keys.
I count the dollars and loose change in the cigar box
and roll my wheelchair to the hopeful side of town.

# Quiet of the Park

I drift off in the quiet of the park where the rustling leaves
keep me company.
I smell the meat on the burning wood of a fire pit.
I used to be hungry, now I just curl up in repose.
Sounds of car tires spin on asphalt, peddling boys on bicycles
churn their spindly legs,
traffic lights change from green to yellow to red for all eternity,
long after I'm gone.
There's a coo from a pigeon, a squawk from an agitated crow.
In the distance, I see a red-tailed hawk tearing up a defenseless
squirrel.
I feel the loss of all the people I know.
The cycle continues with or without them, I guess.
The mushrooming gray clouds in the dusk hover over me
like a warm quilted blanket
and at this moment, I feel safe.

# The Day We Drove to Vegas

I remember that March morning
when we had *huevos rancheros* with Uncle Pete;
when we drove the California and Nevada highways
all the way to Las Vegas.

I remember the Spanish tunes
played by your parents in the backseat,
reminiscing about their own wedding day
in a quiet little church in Santa Paula.

I remember the dusty deserts we passed,
broken down gas stations, abandoned shacks;
the berry stands off the asphalt roads,
Joshua trees huddled together in full bloom.

I remember seeing you smile
when you thought it would never be you
to find such a loving and kind man
in the breath of the sacred angels.

I remember going down long, winding roads,
driving hundreds of miles on low octane
straight through until we hit the jackpot;
the Lucky Little Chapel.

At night, the full moon hung over us,
and seemed to sing from the balcony
as we soon cradled each other in harmony,
cuddling by the fire, wrapped in silk sheets.

We laughed, we kissed,
and remembered the game of Scrabble
that brought us together
from a different culture, a different coast.

I broke your grandmother's wine glass.
You married into a Hebrew tribe
far removed from the Aztec ruins
that you rose above.

While the roulette ball dropped and spun,
we were at the precipice of a new life,
a gamble worth taking.

# Free Speech Table

I approached the folding table,
a Free Speech table,
with much apprehension.
I didn't know what to say.

Ranting about the government
was not my style.
Bitching about my poverty
only made my blood pressure rise.

My bunions hurt, sure, my back was sore
but a lot of other people have it worse.

I had no reason to complain.
My life was going well,
had a warm sleeping bag,
a slow burning candle,
and the moon and stars to keep me company.

So, I stood by the table,
not moving very far,
using my five free minutes
to draw a sun like I did when I was a boy.

It was a big, round sphere
in bright yellow chalk
with a genuine smile
and a thought bubble that read:
"I'm just lucky to be here."

# Pass the Cake

As the chocolate cake passes from one anorexic to the next,
we all take turns shaking our heads, no.
*Not today, I'm full, maybe another day,* I say
as they all sing happy birthday to me
and I blow out the candles.

The cake looks delicious, but the voice
inside my head says you can't afford this, you're much too fat.
And I nod in agreement, *Yes, I am, unbearably so.*

I lick my imaginary lips of creamy chocolate icing,
hunker down on what seems like a feast to many.
The staff says, *Finish everything, let's go, come on.*
I say, *I can't do it.* They say, *One small mouthful at a time.*

But the scary voice in my head always wins out.
I push the plate of food aside and cover my eyes.
My hands feel heavy and my brain grows weary.
I've been fighting this fight for over twenty years.
I've been in and out of group homes and treatment facilities.

No matter how hard I try,
I can never disagree with the voice inside.

# Sandy Queen

Come closer, don't be afraid.
Analyze my sandy queen.
Tell her what you think.
Tell her what it means.

She's there for you, only you
to admire and to photograph.
Shower her, rich tourists
with silver and gold.

Admire her trunk that wraps around
her molded body, a diamond-studded cobra
for warmth and protection
on these cool coastal nights.

She's a mother nursing a calf
that rose from the earth's core.
Her sharp teeth cuts through our lies
and the myths that we hold.

Don't worry, don't be afraid.
It's not a monster; it won't bite.
It only seeks the truth
on this beach of beggar's delight.

# The Charmer

The charmer with a 14-foot Python
around his neck,
lures Sunday strollers like you
to his street corner in Venice Beach.

He tells you that the snake won't bite.
It's tame and loving, like him.
If you gently hold the snake, he'll softly hiss,
wrap its scaly leather around your waist.

At first, you'll feel the coolness of his skin
gradually coiling its passion around you.
Not too tight, but close enough
to let you know of his intentions.

What the charmer doesn't say
is that when the serpent gets hungry,
and if you refuse to feed him,
he won't see you as a friend or an ally.

He will slowly tighten his grip,
squeezing in his predatory manner,
until the beating of your heart
and the sound of your breath
becomes a distant memory.

# Ancient Pyramid

Stanley has just enough strength to pick up the potatoes.
He dumps one burlap bag after another into a large bin,
each Idaho having a different character, a different shape.

The machine churns and catches a potato or two.
They fall onto a rattling conveyor belt
in the quiet darkness of the warehouse floor.

Stanley takes three swigs from the whiskey bottle.
One for his father, another for his mother
and the last swig for a future that might never come.

The potatoes slowly move to their destination,
dropping into five-pound plastic bags,
weighed on a chain-linked scale,
tied and stacked onto a pallet like an ancient pyramid.

After years of bagging potatoes and drinking whiskey,
Stanley's life comes to a grinding halt
as the motor of the bagging machine conks out.

He drops like a sack to the dirty warehouse floor,
squarely on top of the wooden pallet.
He swells up like a rough, knotty potato
and lays there like a bagged Idaho.

# Frayed Blanket

His memories live
in his worn out
woolen blanket
full of moth holes
and frayed at the edges.

He covers himself barely.
His limbs exposed to the cold.
His bruised childhood in Camden
unfolds in murky dreams on broken sidewalks.

His memories are ripped and torn.
He is branded from the iron of regret
by the sins and behaviors
of his mother and father.

# In the Asylum

I remember the voices in the asylum.
The screams bouncing off the walls.
Nurses dropping pills into paper cups.
The aides rolling blood-pressure monitors
down the halls.

All the doors were locked.
The windows were faded.
Visitors had to be approved
and enter at their own risk.

No sharps or shoestrings
for fear that I might
slice my wrists or hang
from a door hinge.

In the dark of the evening
when the intrusive voices grew,
I jumped off the deep end
into a psychotic freefall.

The nurse got out the needles,
brought the leather straps,
a code blue was announced
and I was officially labeled a fucking mess.

They tried to silence me
in a padded room,
sealed my lips in cellophane
with no one to talk to
but myself.

Just a man's eyes I saw
through the narrow slit
of my locked door.

# The Perfect Place

My mother died, but don't worry.
She's all right, doing just fine.
She spends all her days in a quiet wooden box
with me, sleeping on the grass outside.

She's calm now, doesn't say a word,
won't eat a thing, can't move an inch.
Nothing seems to hurt, plenty of fresh air,
warm sunshine and cool California nights.

She's where she wants to be.
Close to her son, by his side
in the woods, deep in the fields.
The perfect place to reside.

Ashes burnt from the past.
Memories drifting in the sea.
No longer flesh and achy bones.
No longer cataracts and hammertoes.

# Coffee Shop Desperado

She sits in the coffee shop
talking to herself,
arguing about things
no one understands.

Past conflicts
that have never been resolved
but still linger in her head.

She drinks from an old coffee cup
tangled in superstition.
She sees her father
at the bottom, her mother
the cream at the top.

She thinks about the children
she's never had.
The babies that fell from her womb
while standing up.

Others see the woman as an outlaw,
a Ma Barker, a bandit queen
about to grab a gun,
start a fistfight,
pull the fire alarm.

Far from dangerous,
far from her home in North Carolina,
she knows she's a desperado;
used to it by now.
She takes her old coffee cup,
unties her imaginary horse,
and rides like Calamity Jane.

# Tattoo Man

The man with a thousand tattoos
shuffles up and down State Street

clothed in a colorful bodysuit.
Skeletal, a striking canvas on display.

He can't sing or dance on Broadway.
Never performed as a circus clown.

He's a moving work of fragmented art.
A thorn in the eye of the beholder,

a magnificent collection of ink and poetry,
a stick figure riding a bike under the moonlight.

# Broken Strings

Mom kept saying that there was nothing wrong
with the two rackets that had broken strings
in her closet.

She wanted us to play on the court together
just like she did with dad,
but I was always too busy.

If I had known that she would die,
I would have taken her
to the courts around the corner
with the sagging nets, puddles
and police sirens in the background.

I wouldn't have acted so ashamed of her
or gotten angry
at her crazy words and behavior
or made fun of her chocolate cake
that lay crumbled on the kitchen table.

If I had known that she would die,
I would have tried harder
to love her as she loved me.

I wouldn't have begged for another mother
or tried to change her.
I would have realized then,
as I do now,
there was never anything wrong
with the two rackets in the closet.

# Waltzing Dreamers

A young homeless couple
living below the poverty line,
among the sirens of despair,
dream of stepping lightly.

They waltz on the cliff of hope,
high in the rich hills of midnight,
moving to the rhythm of the universe,
to a song in their hearts.

Gazing at the light show down below,
slowly, in their own time,
sharing their secrets,
and securing each other's trust.

They find a hidden treasure,
buried beneath their ragged clothes
in the City of Angels, dancing
like Ginger Rogers and Fred Astaire.

# Flying Kings

I watch as two homeless men
play checkers with ease and love
in a laid-back coffee shop.
They drink from their own enamel cups,
stirring fresh cream and sugar into their coffee.

One man triple jumps.
The other gets kinged
as the red and black checkers
by the hands of gnarled fingers
zig and zag, hop and skip.

They play every Wednesday
between six and eight-thirty.
They unfold an old checkerboard
that they bought from Goodwill
and ask the barista to fill their cups with coffee.

One man always triple jumps.
The other always gets kinged.
They play for hours, each waiting his turn,
forgetting about their troubles,
not just a game, but a means to an end.

# About the Author

Mark Tulin was born in Philadelphia, Pennsylvania. He began writing poems as a teenager to cope with asthma and family issues. His poems have been published in *Vita Brevis, The Drabble, Amethyst Review, Spillwords, Leaves of Ink, Scarlet Leaf Review, Amaryllis, Corvus Review, Degenerates for Peace,* among others. His first chapbook of poetry was *Magical Yogis,* published by Prolific Press (2017). Mark is a retired Marriage and Family Therapist who lives in Santa Barbara, California with his wife, Alice.